BUSES IN GREATER MANCHESTER IN THE 1990s

HOWARD WILDE

AMBERLEY

First published 2020

Amberley Publishing
The Hill, Stroud
Gloucestershire, GL5 4EP

www.amberley-books.com

Copyright © Howard Wilde, 2020

The right of Howard Wilde to be identified as
the Author of this work has been asserted in
accordance with the Copyrights, Designs and
Patents Act 1988.

ISBN 978 1 4456 9948 6 (print)
ISBN 978 1 4456 9949 3 (ebook)

British Library Cataloguing in Publication Data.
A catalogue record for this book is available from
the British Library.

Typesetting by Aura Technology and Software
Services, India. Printed in the UK.

Contents

Introduction

The Transport Act 1985 legislated for the deregulation of local bus services in Great Britain outside of London. Its introduction, from 26 October 1986 ('D-day'), brought sweeping change across the British bus industry. In Greater Manchester, the incumbent public-sector transport provider, Greater Manchester PTE, was required to separate its bus operations into an arms-length limited company, for which it remained the sole shareholder. Greater Manchester Transport therefore became Greater Manchester Buses Limited (GM Buses); and the new operator was expected to compete on an open platform with other companies, both new and established. Meanwhile, GMPTE maintained its responsibility for providing timetables and publicity, co-ordinating local rail services, and as managing infrastructure, such as stops, shelters and bus stations. It also subsidised non-profitable bus services in the region, through a process of competitive tendering.

Those early deregulated years, as in other parts of the country, proved to be eventful and, at times, somewhat chaotic. Operators burst onto the scene. Some were existing companies, expanding into the conurbation; some were new emerging groups or firms; some were existing smaller independents, perhaps diversifying into local bus operation for the first time. Operators competed vigorously against each other on commercially registered services. Many also made a niche for themselves, picking up PTE-tendered work.

The turmoil and change continued into the 1990s. Large corporate groups had already begun to establish themselves. Independent operators continued to appear, while others slipped away. Some were rather spectacular in their demise. Meanwhile, GM Buses became something of a political football. The Conservative government wanted it to be privatised, arguing that its size and publicly owned status was causing an anti-competitive situation. On the other hand, the mainly Labour local authorities that made up the controlling Passenger Transport Authority stubbornly held out for it to remain as it was. In the end, the Secretary of State for Transport, John MacGregor, invoked powers under the Act to divide GM into two parts, North and South. This split happened in late 1993. Both companies were then sold in April 1994: the South to staff, under an employee share ownership scheme; the North to a management and employee buyout, with a minority shareholding by financial institutions.

This book primarily concentrates on those bus operators providing such commercial and supported local bus services within Greater Manchester during the 1990s.

In addition to such operations, there were, and still remain, numerous companies who also ran buses and coaches on private hire, excursion and contract work. Indeed, many of the operators who appear in this book also carried out such work.

I'll let the following chapters and pictures tell the rest of the story. I hope that this colourful selection gives you a flavour of those fascinating times.

Howard Wilde,
November 2019

Chapter One
Municipals in the Mix

The council-owned companies that neighboured Greater Manchester all took advantage of commercial and subsidised opportunities within the PTE area during the 1990s. Firstly, there were the Lancashire fleets. Blackburn ran express commuter routes into Manchester, as well as picking up local service work elsewhere. Rossendale was particularly active, establishing a base in Rochdale to operate commercial and GMPTE-contracted services. Then there was Hyndburn, who had gained tendered schools and service work within Greater Manchester.

Burnley & Pendle had picked up some GMPTE contract work from early deregulation – most notably Sunday workings on the Centreline service in city centre Manchester. However, this had waned by the early 1990s, with only odd routes covered in the north of the region.

Meanwhile, from Cheshire, Warrington regularly worked into Altrincham and Leigh from its home area. Finally, from Derbyshire, there was Chesterfield Transport, whose Whites of Calver subsidiary ventured into Greater Manchester on tendered services.

Photographed in Cannon Street, in Manchester, in February 1992, is Blackburn Transport 203 (J418 JBV). This was one of a batch of five Volvo B10M with dual-purpose bodywork by East Lancs.

Blackburn purchased four former London Country Leyland Tigers from Kentish Bus in 1988. They subsequently had them rebuilt with new front and rear ends by East Lancs, to combat the well-known body deficiencies of the ECW B51 coach body. 417 (WPH 141Y) is seen in Manchester, crossing over the junction with Corporation Street, in July 1995.

Hyndburn secured GMPTE contract tenders, gaining both local service and schools work. A base was established for a time at the Bury Council service depot at Bradley Fold. Two Leyland Atlanteans were photographed there in March 1992. Willowbrook-bodied 140 (WWM 920W) was ex-Merseyside PTE; while 207 (NRN 397P), with Park Royal body, was originally a Ribble bus.

Looking very crisp in Hyndburn's distinctive livery is 126 (CWR 526Y), an ex-Yorkshire Woollen ECW-bodied Leyland Olympian. The bus is pictured in Newton Street in Manchester in June 1995, performing a Sunday working of service 701 – normally the preserve of Blackburn during the week.

Hyndburn 57 (WWM 576W) was a former Merseyside PTE Leyland Leopard with Duple bodywork. It is pictured heading towards Piccadilly Station in Manchester in April 1996. Hyndburn eventually sold out to Stagecoach the following September.

Rossendale purchased Leyland Atlanteans from South Yorkshire Transport. Alexander-bodied 191 (JKW 291W) was photographed in Portland Street in Manchester in July 1991. The 17 service to Rochdale was run in competition with GM Buses.

One of Rossendale's more unusual vehicles was this East Lancs-bodied Bristol LHS, 50 (SND 550X) – one of two bought new in 1982. It was captured in Manchester in August 1993, working the express X76. This was initially introduced as a rail-replacement service during Metrolink work on the line to Bury.

Rossendale purchased two imposing Leyland Olympians with East Lancs bodywork to operate their X86 service, branded as Valley Link. The pair had been new to Eastbourne and came to Rossendale via Stevensons of Uttoxeter. 32 (B102 PHC), the second of the two, was photographed in Corporation Street, Manchester in March 1994.

Typical of Leyland Leopards that Rossendale had rebodied by East Lancs in the 1990s is this pair, pictured parked up in Rochdale bus station in August 1994. On the left, 77 (PJI 9177) was originally UGG 369R, new with a Plaxton coach body in 1977 to Ellen Smith; while, on the right, 75 (PJI 9175) had been new to Ribble as WCK 139V, with a Duple body.

Burnley & Pendle had a modest presence in Greater Manchester on tendered work by the start of the nineties. Carrying the company's Whizzard minibus branding is 98 (G98 PCK), a Mercedes 811D with Reeve Burgess body, pictured in Bury Interchange in June 1990.

Warrington operated into Greater Manchester on several routes, including the 19 to Leigh. The town's bus station is the setting for 99 (F99 STB), an East Lancs-bodied Dennis Dominator, in this 1998 view.

Chesterfield had purchased nearby Whites of Calver, an operator who already worked into Greater Manchester. Leyland National 28 (EKY 28V) was transferred to Whites from the main fleet and is seen in otherwise full Chesterfield livery, arriving into Stockport on a Sunday-contracted 199 service in January 1994.

Chapter Two
The General Scene

Eric Booth of Eccles traded as both Ericsway and Lyntown Bus Company, running stage carriage services under the latter name. The Lyntown fleet consisted mainly of Bristol REs, including WSV 134 (ex-EPW 511K), a former Eastern Counties ECW-bodied example. Manchester's Parker Street is the location in March 1990. Booth sold the Lyntown operation and vehicles to Midway a few months later.

Midway YSD 824T was a former Western SMT Alexander-bodied Seddon Pennine 7, and is seen in Manchester city centre in March 1992. Midway initially operated out of Lyntown's Eccles base, before moving to Bradford (the Manchester suburb, not the Yorkshire city), occupying the yard that had previously been used by Citibus.

Midway MLK 665L queues in traffic on Newton Street in Manchester in April 1992. This rather battle-scarred former London Transport Park Royal-bodied Daimler Fleetline had been acquired from Primrose Valley of Filey earlier that year.

The original Bee Line Buzz Company was a brash, high-intensity minibus operation, set up by United Transport International in the early deregulation days. The operation was subsequently sold to Ribble. Then, in an agreement between Ribble's owner, Stagecoach, and Drawlane in October 1989, Ribble's Manchester garage passed to Drawlane, along with Stagecoach's East Midland yard at Tintwistle. Drawlane then formed a revised Bee Line, using a ramshackle collection of inherited and cascaded vehicles. Pictured in Piccadilly, Manchester, in March 1990, is ex-Ribble 1619 (PUF 719M) – a former Southdown Park Royal-bodied Leyland Atlantean. Ribble's livery is still carried, with a yellow front panel added – an arrangement that was sadly all too familiar.

There was still a place at Bee Line for minibuses, despite the transition towards full-sized vehicles. Batches of new Mercedes-Benz 811D with Carlyle and LHE bodywork appeared between 1989 and 1990. Examples of both types are on display in this shot at Bee Line's depot in Oldham in June 1991. Various acquired Park Royal-bodied Atlanteans also make an appearance in the background.

Ex-GM Atlanteans were commonplace in the Bee Line fleet, the operation having initially received an influx from Drawlane-owned London and Country. However, 677 (JDB 117N) had actually been acquired from Stagecoach, having previously seen service with their East Midland and Ribble fleets. The location is Manchester's Stevenson Square in March 1992.

Drawlane purchased Crosville from ATL Holdings in 1989, absorbing most of it into its existing subsidiaries, before selling the remainder to PMT. It created C-Line for Cheshire operations, based in Macclesfield, which also operated into and within Greater Manchester. Crosville's attractive green and cream deregulation livery was retained, but subsequently applied in a different layout. Ex-Crosville Bristol VRT/ECW WTU 471W demonstrates this in Lever Street bus station, Manchester in August 1991.

C-Line received a single example of the Leyland National Greenway in 1992. The Greenway was originally a joint venture between Drawlane subsidiary London & Country and East Lancs, where Leyland Nationals were extensively rebuilt by the Blackburn-based bodybuilder. LFR 875X, a former Ribble National 2, is pictured in Mosley Street in Manchester that May.

Mike Wall was already an established Manchester coach operator when he entered the deregulation fray, initially employing a batch of ex-GM Daimler Fleetlines. He also had this unusual pair of Mercedes 709D with PMT bodies, purchased new in 1988, for local services in Trafford. F545 EJA is pictured, parked up near the company's yard on Ladybarn Road, Fallowfield, in April 1990. Wall would later move to larger premises in Sharston.

Wall's purchased three ex-West Midlands Fleetlines, including Park Royal-bodied GOG 561N. The bus is seen turning from Cannon Street into Corporation Street in Manchester in March 1991. The W46 service mirrored GM Buses' equivalent 46 route.

Wall's developed a taste for DAF vehicles, acquiring both new and youthful second-hand examples. Optare Delta-bodied DAF SB220 H538 YCX is pictured in Altrincham in April 1994. It was one of four that were acquired from OK Travel in 1992, when just one year old. Mike Wall eventually gave up bus work in 1997, selling the service registrations to Stagecoach, but with no vehicles involved.

A most unusual bus in the immaculate fleet of Jim Stones of Glazebury was this Leyland-DAB Tiger Cub, A499 MHG. New as a Leyland demonstrator in 1984, it was one of only two such vehicles built for the UK market. Stones would later end up acquiring the other bus as well, namely former United B500 MPY. Elderly passengers queue to board at Leigh bus station in May 1990.

Irwell Valley Motor Services traded as Eccles Grey and operated minibuses in the main, serving the Salford area. GLJ 474N was one of their larger vehicles, an ECW-bodied Bristol LH, new to Hants & Dorset in 1974. Financial difficulties caused the company to cease trading suddenly in 1993.

Stott's of Oldham had been operating coaches and some buses since the 1950s and entered full-heartedly into local commercial bus work at deregulation. The initial bedrock of that operation was a batch of ex-GM Daimler Fleetlines. Stott's 9 (YNA 303M), a Northern Counties-bodied example from 1974, is pictured negotiating the roundabout at the Broadoak Hotel in Ashton in April 1991.

Terry Wild set up Central Coaches in Oldham in 1980, and began the 407 service in 1987, running between Manchester, Oldham and Denshaw. Various buses were operated, many of which ran with little alteration to previous operators' colours. JWU 254N, a former West Yorkshire PTE Leyland Leopard/Plaxton, was still very much in Stott's livery in this view in Manchester in March 1990.

Stuart's had been a modest-sized coach operator, before expanding into stage carriage work at deregulation. 110 (NRG 175M) was a former Aberdeen Corporation Alexander-bodied Leyland Atlantean; one of five of the same type purchased from various sources. The location is Alexandra Street in Hyde in April 1990, near Stuart's yard of the time. Sadly, within six months of this photo, 110 was deroofed in a low-bridge accident and written off.

Established in 1980, Citibus grew to become a significant player in the Manchester deregulated bus scene. Backbone of the early deregulation fleet was a selection of former Preston Corporation Leyland Panthers, acquired from Isle of Man National Transport. A few of these survived into the early nineties, including Seddon-bodied 34 (RTF 434L), pictured on Oldham Street, Manchester, in May 1990.

Citibus bought a considerable number of ex-South Yorkshire Leyland Atlanteans, with various bodywork, from the late 1980s onwards. Several of these were converted to single door in the company's workshop at their Chadderton depot. Roe-bodied 618 (VET 618S) demonstrates the conversion as it turns into Piccadilly in June 1991.

Shearings was and remains a major operator of coach holidays, but they also diversified in a large way into local bus work at deregulation. Leyland Lynx 42 (F42 ENF) was one of twelve bought new, seen in Bury Interchange on a grey day in June 1990.

Shearings eventually gave up local bus work, and operations and vehicles passed to Timeline Travel of Leigh at the start of 1992. Shearings livery was retained. Pictured in Cannon Street, in Manchester, in January of that year, was RSR 846H – an elderly Plaxton-bodied Leyland Leopard that had been new to Trent as ACH 142H in April 1970. The unrelated Scottish destination is noteworthy.

A scene from July 1992 on High Street in central Manchester, featuring Timeline 136 (HOR 316N), a former Portsmouth Alexander-bodied Leyland Atlantean. The bus was one of five such vehicles inherited from the Shearings business.

The London AEC Routemaster became a surprising deregulation weapon for many operators throughout the country. GM Buses took ten for use along the lively Wilmslow Road corridor, branding them as 'Piccadilly Line' in London-style red. 2205 (618 DYE) is pictured at the West Didsbury terminus on the last day of operation in June 1990. However, it wouldn't be the last time that Routemasters appeared on the Wilmslow Road, as we will see later.

One of GM Buses' infamous 'scuds', nicknamed after the missiles employed by Iraqi dictator Saddam Hussein during the first Gulf War. These MCW Metroriders were hired in from West Midlands Travel and used to target competitors, running as duplicates of existing duties. F676 YOG, still in West Midlands' colours, turns into Church Street, Manchester, in February 1992.

GM Buses inherited three converted Leyland Atlantean open toppers at deregulation. Although intended for private hire, it wasn't unknown for them to appear on regular service as well. Northern Counties-bodied 4172 (VBA 172S) is pictured as such in Corporation Street in Manchester in June 1993. Unfortunately, it was written off two years later, following accident damage sustained after being stolen.

Thirty Northern Counties-bodied Dennis Dominators passed to GM Buses at deregulation, all eventually allocated to their Princess Road depot. 2015 (B915 TVR) is seen in Parker Street, Manchester, in September 1993, carrying branding for an Airport service, although not actually operating on it at the time. It had also received coach seating in lieu of the previous bus seats.

Hulme Hall Coaches of Cheadle Hulme, Stockport, had its origins in the 1970s as a department providing pupil transport within the school of the same name. It was reconstituted as a separate company in the 1980s. At deregulation it registered its school journeys commercially, as well as undertaking private hire and contract work. Ex-GMPTE Daimler Fleetline/Northern Counties CSU 917 (ex-GDB 165N) and former Crosville Bristol VRT/ECW WTU 490W are pictured in the yard in June 1991.

Mayne of Clayton was unique among Manchester independents in having operated local bus services uninterrupted since the 1920s. Operations expanded considerably at deregulation. 21 (A101 DPB) was a Dennis Falcon with Wadham Stringer bodywork, pictured in Manchester in September 1991. The bus had been new to Alder Valley in 1983, and was rebodied by the same bodybuilder in 1987, following major fire damage.

Leafy surroundings on Wood Lane in Ashton, in May 1993, with Mayne 30 (ULS 663T) heading out towards Mossley on the 235 service. The bus was one of three former Scottish Bus Group ECW-bodied Leyland Fleetlines purchased, having been new to Alexander (Midland) in 1979. A temporary malfunction of the destination equipment has necessitated the use of window numerals on this occasion.

Mayne was an enthusiastic user of former London Transport DMS-class Leyland Fleetlines, taking its first three in the years before deregulation, followed by more, mainly B20-types, in the early nineties. Park Royal-bodied 35 (THX 555S) was captured in Ashton, on a wintery day in February 1996.

Vale operated from a yard in Cheetham in Manchester, not far from the Manchester Museum of Transport. Captured parked in the road outside, in December 1991, was this ECW-bodied Bristol RE, EHU 383K, new originally to Bristol Omnibus.

Vale's SPW 105R was a former Eastern Counties Leyland Leopard/Plaxton, new in 1977. New Metrolink tram tracks can be seen in this shot in Manchester's Piccadilly bus station in March 1992.

Cooper (Dennis's) of Ashton-under-Lyne entered deregulation running minibuses mainly, but also with some full-sized vehicles. J23 GCX, a DAF SB220 with Optare Delta bodywork, was acquired new in September 1991. It is pictured a month later, parked near their small garage in the town. Dennis's subsequently set up bases at different venues in nearby Dukinfield.

Typical of the minibuses purchased by Dennis's was L680 GNA, a Mercedes-Benz 709D with Plaxton bodywork, pictured when new in January 1994. The minibus is in Manchester, Piccadilly, working an outbound trip to Ashton on service 216, originally a trolleybus service in corporation days.

Dennis's purchased Leyland Nationals from Isle of Man National Transport in 1994, including this former East Kent example, which had been MAN 19D in its Manx days. Despite being re-registered NFN 62M upon return to the UK, the bus had actually been new as NFN 71M. The original NFN 62M had previously been scrapped on the island. The driver gives a friendly wave in this view on Market Street, Manchester, in October that year.

PMT set up a small base in Bredbury, Stockport, under their Red Rider brand, to work schools and tendered work. 2169 (A169 VFM), a former Crosville Leyland Olympian/ECW, is pictured there on a wet day in January 1992.

Stevensons secured GMPTE-tendered service work in 1991, operating from bases in Stockport under the trading name of Pacer. Ex-South Yorkshire Transport Optare-bodied Dennis Domino 227 (C54 HDT) carries a partial repaint, with the previous red portion painted green, in this shot in Newton Street, Manchester, in January 1992.

In addition to Pacer-branded mini- and midi-buses, Stevensons also drafted in full-size single-deckers to assist. 101 (DUH 76V) was a former Rhymney Valley Leyland Leopard with an East Lancs body, captured in Manchester in April 1992.

Roger Jarvis and Alan Turner, two former Shearings managers, set up Blue Bus in 1991, based in Horwich. A distinctive vehicle owned was 19 (BWU 691H) – a Seddon-bodied short Leyland Leopard that had been new to Todmorden in 1969, and which had also had a more recent stint with Shearings. The bus is turning into Piccadilly, in Manchester, in this June 1992 view.

Two former Midland Red Leyland Leopards with Blue Bus – 43 (GOH 353N) and 22 (JHA 229L) – are pictured in Blackhorse Street in Bolton in April 1993. Both feature bodywork by Marshall in the typical BET style.

Blue Bus 40 (WCW 310R) was a Leyland Leopard new to Lancaster in 1977. The classic lines of the Alexander Y-type body are nicely demonstrated in this view in Withy Grove, in Manchester, in August 1996.

Blue Bus 12 (LHL 246P), a smart Leyland Leopard with Alexander T-type bodywork, pictured on Blackhorse Street, in Bolton, in April 1994. The bus was new to Yorkshire Traction in 1976.

Keeley and Shepley, later Keeley alone, traded as Tame Valley from a base in Hyde. A fine vehicle in the fleet was C56 (XPK 56T), a Duple-bodied AEC Reliance, new to London Country in 1978. It is seen in Church Street in Manchester in July 1992.

Tame Valley initially had this former West Midlands PTE Alexander-bodied Volvo Ailsa on loan from a Barnsley dealer in June 1992, still in the livery of London Buses' Harrow Bus operation. In the end, the bus was purchased outright, and 53 (JOV 753P) is seen here two months later in Piccadilly, Manchester, looking very smart in full fleet colours.

Ralph Bullock set up business in 1928 in Cheadle, initially as a haulage operator, but soon diversified into coach operation. At deregulation, the firm initially had a fairly modest number of buses for schools and tendered work, but this grew as competitive work developed. One of many different buses operated was this ex-London Transport Leyland Fleetline/Park Royal, THX 563S, captured in Mosley Street, Manchester, in January 1993. Bullock re-engineered the bus substantially, replacing the distinctive B20-type back end with a conventional Fleetline engine bustle, and repowering with a Gardner 6LXB engine.

North Western Road Car Company Limited – sharing the same name as the famous predecessor, but not actually the same legal entity – was set up to take control of the Merseyside portion of Ribble prior to deregulation. After D-day and under Drawlane ownership, operations spread east, with a presence in south Manchester from a base in Altrincham. Two former NBC-era ECW-bodied Leyland Olympians are pictured, wearing the company's distinctive asymmetric livery, in Manchester's Piccadilly bus station in July 1993. On the left is ex-Crosville 661 (A151 UDM), standing alongside ex-Ribble 613 (B153 TRN).

British Bus – as Drawlane had become in November 1992 – transferred control of Macclesfield depot from C-Line to sister company Midland Red North at the start of 1993. Allocated there was a trio of Plaxton-bodied Scania K93 that had been new to Happy Days of Woodseaves three years earlier. 1110 (G610 CFA) carries MRN livery with dual fleetnames in this shot in Manchester Piccadilly bus station that January.

Midland Red North 1904 (EEH 904Y) is pictured on Mosley Street in Manchester in September 1993, returning to Macclesfield. The retro Midland Red colours had initially been applied as a commemorative livery on selected vehicles only, before eventually being adopted as standard.

Mybus began operations in 1991, based in Hadfield in Derbyshire. They initially competed against GM on the established 211 service from Manchester out to Hyde, Hattersley and Glossop. OTO 541M was a former Nottingham Leyland Atlantean/East Lancs and is pictured in central Manchester in March 1993 in a rather sorry state. Mybus eventually fell foul of the traffic commissioners and operations ceased for a time. The company later returned on a smaller scale, running along the Wilmslow Road, mainly on evening and night services.

Paul Hughes was the archetypal 'one-man band', a former GM Buses employee who set up Atherton Bus Company, operating service 592 between Bolton and Shakerley. GNS 672N was one of two former Greater Glasgow PTE Alexander-bodied Leyland Atlanteans owned, and is captured at speed, Bolton-bound, in July 1993, with the proprietor at the wheel.

Two Ribble Leyland Nationals – 725 (UHG 725R) and 697 (SCK 697P) – wait side-by-side at the lights on Victoria Bridge Street in April 1992, having just crossed over the Irwell from Salford into Manchester. Although Ribble had been owned by Stagecoach since 1988, both buses still retain the original Ribble deregulation livery of red and grey.

Stagecoach invested in new vehicles for Ribble's inter-urban routes, as it did throughout the country. Plaxton-bodied Dennis Javelins appeared on the X43 between Manchester and Burnley and the X25 to Blackburn. 149 (L149 BFV), new in November 1993, is pictured in Manchester the following March, complete with typical branding of the time.

As mentioned earlier, Routemasters made a return to Wilmslow Road, this time courtesy of Mancunian Bus Company. Mancunian had the same owners as Midway but ran on a separate licence. YTS 973A (ex-17 CLT) had, like many RMs, seen prior service in Scotland, on this occasion with Strathtay. The bus is pictured on Princess Street, Manchester, in March 1993. Midway eventually folded through financial woes later in the year. Operations continued for a while on a reduced Mancunian licence, using a handful of used double-deckers, including a few of the remaining Routemasters, before that too ceased.

Pennine Blue – full registered name United Provincial Services Limited – commenced operation in 1990, based initially in Ashton and later in nearby Dukinfield. They will mainly be remembered for their fondness for the Bristol RE. A particularly venerable specimen was 1 (NLJ 821G), a dual-doored, flat-screened ECW-bodied example, new to Hants & Dorset in 1968. It is seen at the junction of Curzon Road and Kings Road in Ashton in July 1993.

Former Leeds Roe-bodied Leyland Atlantean 7574 (SUG 574M) was acquired by Pennine Blue from Yorkshire Rider. Its previous ownership is still evident as it powers past terraced housing on Whiteacre Road in Ashton in May 1993. Rider's green was overpainted blue, with the cream left untouched and YR markings still visible.

Liveley of Marple traded as Rose Hill Coaches and operated from a yard adjacent to the railway station of that name. Former London Transport Leyland National BYW 362V – still in London red – is pictured ascending Wellington Road South, in Stockport, on a sunny day in June 1993.

Wigan Bus Company commenced operations in 1993 and evoked local heritage by adopting Wigan Corporation livery. They initially used a mixture of Leyland Nationals and ex-London DMS-class Leyland Fleetlines. Park Royal-bodied Fleetline 12 (OJD 462R) was photographed in the town's bus station in July that year.

Finglands was one of the longest established Manchester independents, with origins going back to 1907. Former GM Atlanteans and Fleetlines had been the mainstay of the fleet from deregulation onwards. 1723 (RJA 703R) was a Northern Counties-bodied example acquired from East Kent, pictured in Princess Street, Manchester, in August 1993.

Finglands Leyland Leopard 237 (HIL 7747) had been new as an Alexander-bodied export demonstrator for Singapore in 1979, registered SBS 6791L. Finglands acquired it in August 1995, it having been owned by Woods of Mirfield and Allander of Milngavie in the interim. It received this Plaxton body while with Allander.

EYMS Group, the owners of East Yorkshire, purchased Finglands in 1992. Early acquisitions by the new owners were five MCW Metrobuses that had been new to London Buses' Harrow operation in 1988. 1730 (E480 UOF) heads into central Manchester on Oxford Street in November 1995.

A one-off in the Bee Line fleet was 684 (YDS 651S), an Alexander-bodied Leyland Atlantean, purchased from Graham's of Paisley in 1990. In this August 1993 shot, 684 has arrived in Ashton from Rochdale on the 409 service. Rossendale was negotiating to take over Bee Line's Rochdale garage at this time, and this and several other Bee Line buses had had fleet names removed in readiness. In the end, the takeover never happened and 684 remained with Bee Line.

Heaton of Hindley Green operated mainly minibuses and had invested in new vehicles in the early years of deregulation. However, something a bit older and larger was YFR 497R – a former Ribble Duple-bodied Leyland Leopard – pictured in Leigh in September 1993. Operations ceased a few years later when the company lost its operator's licence.

Bolton-based Evag Cannon ran buses in the town during the early 1990s. A number of Leyland Nationals was operated, along with some coaches, in this short-lived venture. Pictured in Deansgate, in September 1993, is ex-Alder Valley TPE 160S, named *Robin Hood*. Note the sticker promoting Manchester's ultimately unsuccessful bid for the 2000 Olympic Games.

Stuart's acquired MCW Metrobus 125 (EWF 469V) from Stevensons in 1993. It was photographed leaving Manchester for Hyde and Newton on Stuart's 209 service in August of that year. The bus had been new to South Yorkshire PTE in 1980.

Stuarts purchased three former South Yorkshire PTE Leyland Atlanteans with bodywork by Marshall in January 1994. The trio had come from Stewart of Stevenston, a member of the Ayrshire Bus Owners (A1 Service) co-operative. 126 (JKW 310W) is seen in Stuart's then new premises in Dukinfield two months later, displaying a rather rudimentary single-door conversion it had received while in Scotland. Despite the establishment of this new base and growing investment in new vehicles, Stuart ceased operating all bar a few coaches in 1997. Its operating licence allowance had been halved because of maintenance issues. Then there was an accident involving a double-decker on a schools contract, allocated in error to a single-deck-only route, resulting in roof damage from overhead trees. Thankfully there were no injuries. The PTE revoked all of Stuart's contracts and the incident made the local television news at the time.

Citibus was purchased by Lynton Travel Group, owners of County Bus of Harlow, in July 1993. Several second-hand purchases entered the fleet, together with examples transferred in-house. A batch of former London Country Leyland Nationals was acquired from Southend, including 783 (HPF 309N), pictured in Princess Street that September. Southend's livery was retained, with a yellow band eventually replacing red. This scheme was also adopted elsewhere in the fleet.

Peter Walsh, based in Middleton, operated as both JP Executive and City Nippy, before eventually becoming JP Travel. Wright-bodied Mercedes 709D K123 AJA is seen in Mosley Street, Manchester, in September 1993.

JP Travel H84 PTG is pictured in Cannon Street, Manchester, in January 1996. This Optare-bodied Mercedes 811D had been new to Bebb of Llantwit Fadre in 1991 and was one of a pair acquired from nearby Wall's in September 1995.

The Dunstan family established Bluebird Bus and Coach in 1988, primarily running minibuses, but also branching out into larger vehicles. Operations were initially based in Moston, before moving a short distance into Middleton. Pictured in Manchester, in October 1993, is LBU 607V – one of two Alexander-bodied Leyland Leopards acquired from Burnley & Pendle. It was originally registered YHG 16V, this mark being sold for use on a private car. Bluebird later had both buses rebodied by East Lancs.

Looking smart in Bluebird's blue and white livery is 54 (VNN 54Y), an ex-Trent Leyland Leopard with Willowbrook body. The location is Stevenson Square, Manchester, in September 1995.

Whyatt (Glossopdale) of Glossop commenced operations in 1992, securing tendered work in both Derbyshire and Greater Manchester. Minibuses were operated in the main; but one notable full-size exception was C203 GKR, a rather brutal Wright-bodied Bedford YMT that had been new to Maidstone Borough Council in 1986. The bus is pictured in Wellington Road South in Stockport, heading out to Glossop, in March 1994. Glossopdale would later relocate into Greater Manchester proper, ultimately settling in Dukinfield.

Pennine Blue was purchased by PMT in November 1993 and, within days of that, Badgerline Holdings acquired PMT. A new company, Pennine Blue Limited, was formed, with the previous Pennine Blue owners kept on as managers. Typical of PMT vehicles drafted in was ECW-bodied Bristol VRT YBF 685S, pictured in Ashton in April 1994. Blue has replaced red in a partial repaint; and a pseudo-GMT fleet number, 1485, is carried, an indulgence carried over from independent days.

Arrowline of Knutsford, Cheshire, traded as Star Line and gained tendered work in Cheshire and Greater Manchester. Plaxton-bodied Dennis Dart K877 UDB was new in September 1992 and is pictured in Altrincham Interchange in April 1994. The company was eventually taken over by British Bus.

PMT took central control of the Pennine business in 1994, with the existing management team accepting redundancy. PMT also took the opportunity to merge the Red Rider operation at Bredbury into the Pennine business. From there came DOG748 (EWY 78Y), one of two ex-West Yorkshire PTE Roe-bodied Leyland Olympians, inherited by PMT from its takeover of Turners of Brown Edge. A youthful Dennis Dart/Plaxton is also pictured in this August 1994 view in Ashton bus station.

Reliance of Ashton-under-Lyne was a small operator, who gained GMPTE contract work for a short time. GHM 782N was a former London Transport Daimler Fleetline/MCW, and is pictured in Denton, working service 324 to Stockport, one Sunday in May 1994.

Stott's purchased three former Central SMT Dennis Dominators with Alexander bodywork from Clydeside Scottish in 1993. TYS 256W is pictured in Ashton in June 1994, loading passengers outside the former fire station on Wellington Road.

A sunny summer day in Oldham in June 1994. Stott's AFY 183X, a former Merseyside PTE Willowbrook-bodied Leyland Atlantean, works service 398 to Stalybridge. Stott gave up local bus work in 1997 in a deal with First Manchester, concentrating instead on coaching and schools' contracts for a time, before returning in 2003.

Daly Bus ran minibus services for a time in the 1990s, based in Eccles. One full-size vehicle in their fleet was JMB 328T, a former Crosville Duple-bodied Leyland Leopard. The coach is pictured working an evening service on the 42, in this view on Oxford Street, Manchester, in June 1994.

Martin Bull traded as Bu-Val, operating minibuses in and around Rochdale. Photographed in Rochdale bus station, in August 1994, was D905 MDB – a former GM Buses Northern Counties-bodied Dodge S56, which had been acquired from Merseyside Transport. The Merseymini legend is still visible above the windscreen.

Captured in the revised double-deck livery of the new GM Buses North is 4975 (DWH 691W), a Northern Counties-bodied Leyland Fleetline that had originally been new to Lancashire United Transport. The bus is seen in Corporation Street, Manchester, in August 1994. Note the previous GM Buses name still remains in the upper-deck window.

Stalwarts of GM's operation in the Bolton and Wigan areas were the remnants of a batch of former Lancashire United Transport Plaxton-bodied Leyland Leopards. Despite appearances to the contrary, 462 (MTE 30R) was in fact a GM Buses North vehicle in this shot on Portland Street, in Manchester, in May 1994.

GM Buses North purchased Citibus from Lynton Group in February 1995, initially operating it as a separate unit. Gradually, operations were merged and some Citibus vehicles received full GMN livery. One such bus was 1732 (CWG 732V), a former South Yorkshire Alexander-bodied Leyland Atlantean, pictured in Stevenson Square, Manchester, in June that year.

GM Buses took delivery of four Leyland Lynx in December 1986, with all passing to GM Buses North. The first, by then numbered 1401 (D501 LNA), is pictured in Bolton, Moor Lane bus station, in January 1996. All were rebuilt to rectify bodywork deficiencies, including adding replacement aluminium wheel-arches and Northern Counties front panels.

GM Buses South 1466 (H466 GVM) was one of five Northern Counties-bodied Scania N113DRB purchased by GM Buses in 1991. It carries the GMS Buses identity adopted by the new company in this view in Ashton in October 1994. The congratulatory notice from advertising agency Buspak relates to GMS's sale to its employees that April.

Typical of the many GM Standard-class Atlanteans in the GM Buses South fleet was 4495 (SND 495X). This NCME-bodied example was captured in a country setting, near Daisy Nook, in September 1995, heading from Ashton to Southern Cemetery on the circuitous 169 route.

British Bus rationalised its north-west operations during 1994, bringing Bee Line under North Western management control. All Manchester operations became Bee Line as a result, and an adaptation of North Western's diagonal livery was introduced. Former North Western 642 (G642 CHF), a Volvo B10M Citybus/East Lancs, is seen laying over in York Street, in Manchester, in August that year.

British Bus leased a batch of MCW Metrobuses from West Midlands Travel in 1994, for use by Bee Line and North Western. Bee Line 811 (GOG 263W) is pictured on a wet day in Oldham in January 1995, sporting a later version of Bee Line livery.

West Midlands Travel eventually required the return of their leased Metrobuses from British Bus. They offered instead a batch of Leyland Nationals, which had been refurbished and fitted with DAF engines. Bee Line 403 (MIL 5573, ex-TOE 487N) demonstrates the colourful standard livery of the time, with joint fleet names, in this July 1996 view in Piccadilly bus station, Manchester.

South Manchester was set up by the original owners of Pennine Blue. The Bristol RE theme continued, with the arrival of two East Lancs-bodied examples from Rossendale. However, 12 (JDK 912P) was actually on hire to Tame Valley in this shot in Penny Meadow, in Ashton, in August 1994. Both operators shared the same canal-side yard in Hyde and such loans were not uncommon at the time. As for Tame Valley, Glossopdale eventually took over their services in 1995. No vehicles were involved in the deal.

Rothwell of Dukinfield 41 (PBD 41R), an ex-Northampton Alexander-bodied Bristol VRT, is pictured at the Parrs Wood terminus in East Didsbury in May 1995. Rothwell was associated with South Manchester and pitched in on their operations on his own operator's licence, using the same green and cream livery. Another operator, Mayall (later Mayall & Walsh), also enjoyed a similar relationship. The VRT eventually passed to Mayall that December.

South Manchester 52 (PTD 652S) is pictured passing Manchester University precinct on Oxford Road in June 1996. The bus had been acquired from Chesterfield and was originally new to GMPTE-owned Lancashire United in 1977. The traffic commissioners eventually revoked South Manchester's operator-licence because of numerous maintenance failings.

Trent purchased five Alexander (Belfast)-bodied Volvo B10Ms in November 1994, primarily for their Trans-Peak service between Nottingham and Manchester. 52 (M52 PRA) approaches the Manchester terminus in this view in Fairfield Street in January 1995.

Yorkshire Rider, the deregulation successor of West Yorkshire PTE, ran into Greater Manchester on several routes. 5161 (F161 XYG), a Leyland Olympian with Northern Counties body, arrives into Rochdale bus station on the long-established 589 service in August 1994. Note the Todmorden coat of arms on the radiator, carried since the vehicle was new.

Bullock was fortunate to obtain two new Volvo Olympians in January 1995, following a mix-up that saw short- instead of long-wheelbase chassis being bodied at East Lancs, leading to their rejection by intended owner Delaine of Bourne. M788 NBA is pictured in May that year, crossing the boundary from Parrs Wood, Manchester, into Stockport.

Pictured in October 1995, passing the now-demolished BBC studios on Oxford Road, Manchester, is Bullock's JFT 413X. The bus was one of two Alexander-bodied Scania BR112DH acquired from Busways that had been new to Busways' predecessor, Tyne and Wear PTE, in 1982.

Piccadilly bus station, Manchester, in January 1996, and Bullock's HFM 804N puts in a turn on local service work. The Plaxton-bodied Leyland Leopard was by then a veteran in the fleet, having been new to them twenty-one years previously.

Mayne celebrated their seventy-fifth anniversary in 1995 and marked the occasion by having one of two new Scania N113DRB/East Lancs painted in the company's original maroon and turquoise bus livery. 11 (M211 NDB) looks resplendent in this view in Ashton that July.

Mayne purchased examples of East Lancs' Cityzen body on Scania N113 chassis, taking its first four in August 1996. 2 (P102 HNC) is pictured on its first day in service, passing through Stevenson Square in Manchester.

Lofty of Bridge Trafford, Cheshire, operated the X3 between Chester and Manchester for a time, under contract to Cheshire County Council. C853 EML was one of a number of unusual short Plaxton Bustler-bodied Volvo B10M operated and is pictured leaving Manchester in August 1995. The buses had been new to Ralphs of Langley in 1986, for use on Heathrow Airport shuttle work.

British Bus bought Stevensons in 1994 and placed it under Midland Red North management. Macclesfield depot passed to Stevensons as part of the rearrangement, marking a return of their vehicles into Manchester, following the closure of the Pacer operation a few years earlier. A notable performer was 99 (Q246 EVT), the very first example of what became the Leyland Olympian (chassis number B45-01). The bus had originally been a Leyland development vehicle and was purchased by Stevensons in 1984.

Finglands received five Volvo Olympians with Alexander's Royale bodywork in August 1995. Four of these were new vehicles, while the fifth was a former demonstrator. One of the new examples, 1743 (N743 VBA), is pictured outside Manchester's Royal Exchange when new.

Finglands acquired four Alexander-bodied Volvo B10M Citybuses from Trent in August 1999, adding to one similar example bought new. 1713 (G613 OTV) was photographed in Portland Street, Manchester, in September that year.

One of the real characters of the Greater Manchester deregulation era was John Whitehead, who operated as Sports Tours and later Pioneer, based in Smithybridge, near Rochdale. MSL 155X was a Willowbrook-bodied Leyland Leopard, seen in Cannon Street, Manchester, in October 1995. Closer observation reveals a rather odd seating layout, with all passenger seats rearward-facing.

A star of the Whitehead fleet was RDV 419H, a semi-preserved Bristol RE with ECW coach body, which was operated in full Royal Blue livery. This view from March 1996 shows the 1970 vehicle turning into High Street, Manchester, bound for Rochdale.

An unusual vehicle for North Western was 857 (G644 EVN), a CVE Omni, in use in Wigan on a GMPTE-supported Easylink community access service. This bus had been new to Wigan Community Transport in 1990, as part of a larger GMPTA-supported ring-and-ride network.

Following the collapse of Heaton's, British Bus set up Leigh Line to take over the services. 244 (CBV 767S), a Leyland National transferred from the North Western fleet, takes on passengers in Wigan bus station in January 1996. The livery is essentially that of Bee Line, the name used also reflecting that connection. The National had originally been new to Ribble in 1977.

Finch of Higher Ince, near Wigan, did not operate local bus services, instead running private hire, contract and schools work. Their definite stand-out vehicle was MJA 893G, a former Stockport Corporation East Lancs-bodied Leyland Titan PD3, new in 1969. This half-cab veteran is pictured leaving the depot on a schools contract in June 1996.

Sam Tandy (Checkmate) of Mossley was an early deregulation participant, initially running GMPTE-tendered service 352 between Ashton and Denshaw. Captured in Ashton, in March 1996, was E184 CNE, a 1988 Northern Counties-bodied Iveco, one of ten that had been leased short-term to GM Buses when new. Checkmate's local bus operations ceased shortly after this picture was taken, before recommencing in 1998. The licence was by then in the name of Tandy's partner, Bernadette Poole.

Stagecoach invested in articulated coaches for several inter-urban services, including a batch for Ribble for use on the X43 and X61 services from Manchester. The experiment was short-lived, with manoeuvrability being an issue in several locations. 101 (P973 UBV), a Plaxton-bodied Volvo B10M, waits over in Major Street outside Chorlton Street coach station, when new in August 1996.

A vandal attack at Ribble's Bolton garage, just after Christmas 1996, led to Stagecoach sourcing replacement buses from elsewhere in the group. This included a batch of Alexander-bodied Dennis Lances from London, which moved north in 1997. 186 (J106 WSC) is pictured in Portland Street in Manchester that April.

Glossopdale M86 DEW was the second of two Marshall-bodied Dennis Darts, purchased in December 1994. The bus is captured in Darnton Road in Ashton in September 1997, working a tendered Sunday journey on the 389 service.

Glossopdale obtained some double-deckers in 1997 for schools contracts gained. Former GM Northern Counties-bodied Leyland Atlantean NIL 9311 (originally ANA 609Y) is pictured in Hyde bus station in June 1998. By this time, Stagecoach Manchester was providing assistance, lending Glossopdale vehicles, primarily for schools work. Glossopdale eventually sold out to Stagecoach in early 1999.

Bluebird DEM 760Y, a former Merseyside Alexander-bodied MCW Metrobus, is pictured turning into Piccadilly in April 1997. Its predecessor's fleet number is still carried.

Stagecoach obtained full control of Burnley & Pendle in March 1997, after a somewhat acrimonious stand-off where Burnley Council initially refused to sell its 50 percent share. Stagecoach then transferred some Ribble operations to their new purchase, including the X43 service. 1301 (E101 JFV), an Alexander-bodied Volvo B10M Citybus, new in 1988, is pictured in Portland Street, Manchester, in January 1998. Burnley & Pendle livery is still carried, including branding for an unrelated Blackpool service.

Manchester operator Ashall's introduced a city open-top tour in 1998. RMS 396W was an ex-Alexander (Midland) Duple-bodied Leyland Leopard, specially converted for the occasion. Greater Manchester PTE had banned double-deck open-top operation on safety grounds, citing the proximity of Metrolink overhead wiring on some sections of the route. Although satisfactory income was generated, Ashall's decided not to proceed beyond that first season, choosing instead to concentrate on regular coach operations. They also later gained GMPTE-tendered local service work.

We are well into Arriva ownership in this shot on Victoria Street, Manchester, in June 1998; but Bee Line 390 (B51 XFV) still looks very much as before. This East Lancs-bodied Dennis Falcon was one of two new to Hyndburn. Both came into British Bus ownership following the takeover of South Lancs Transport in St Helens. 390 was eventually exported to Malta.

UK North were the successors to Mybus. Based initially in Hadfield and later in Gorton, they built up a considerable presence, notably on the Wilmslow Road. SND 506X was one of many former GM Leyland Atlanteans owned and is pictured in Manchester's Piccadilly bus station in July 1998.

EKA 226Y is seen with Dootson (B&D Coaches) of Leigh, leaving the Trafford Centre in December 1998. This Duple-bodied Dennis Lancet was one of a batch of ten, new to Merseyside PTE in 1983.

Gilligan and Wilson (Nova-Scotia) of Winsford, Cheshire, started operating commercial services in Greater Manchester in 1998, linked in with schools tenders they had gained in the Altrincham area. They had also won some GMPTE-tendered local service work using minibuses. Captured in Portland Street, in Manchester, in July 1998, was WJI 6162 (ex-ORJ 71W), a former Stagecoach Manchester MCW Metrobus that had been new to Greater Manchester Transport in 1981. Arriva acquired the Nova-Scotia business in 1999, leading to its departure from the Manchester scene.

South Lancs Travel of Atherton was a resurrection in Greater Manchester of the previous South Lancs Transport, which had been based in St Helens in Merseyside. Duple-bodied Dennis Javelin G621 CPS was a well-travelled bus that had been new to Leask of Lerwick, Shetland, in 1990. It is seen leaving the Trafford Centre in August 1999.

South Lancs Travel's official name was Green Triangle Buses Limited, and it was this name that was initially used at the start of operations. HIL 7467 – pictured at the Trafford Centre in December 1998 – was a Volvo B10M, rebodied by East Lancs in 1991. It had originally been FUA 387Y, a Plaxton-bodied coach, new to Wallace Arnold in 1983.

The Coachmasters of Rochdale gained schools contracts in north-west Greater Manchester in 1999, and registered commercial services to link in with them. Typical of vehicles operated was former Hull G805 JRH – a 1989 Scania N113 with East Lancs body – pictured in Wigan in September that year. The operation was later acquired by First, who ran it as a dedicated school bus unit from a yard in Ince.

A non-blue Blue Bus. 47 (M647 RCP) was one of two Northern Counties-bodied DAF DB250 that were acquired in all-over white. The bus is pictured in Bradshawgate in Bolton in March 1996. Both vehicles were eventually treated to full Blue Bus livery.

Very smart additions to the Blue Bus fleet were five East Lancs-bodied Volvo Olympians, purchased between 1998 and 1999. 45 (S45 SNB) is pictured in Wigan bus station in September 1999, carrying the company's later, lighter blue livery.

Chapter Three
Some Notable Skirmishes

The state of competition in Greater Manchester was always lively, but clashes between some of the 'big boys' raised things to a different level. Such was the spat between the two neighbouring former PTE operators. Merseyside Transport (Merseybus) launched into Greater Manchester in various forms, having recently been sold to its own management under a holding company, MTL Trust Holdings Limited. This led to a corresponding backlash from GM Buses and its North and South successors, dishing out retaliatory action in Merseyside.

Elsewhere, there was Stagecoach's robust invasion into south Manchester, which led to GM Buses South hitting back on Stagecoach's express services into Lancashire.

MTL commenced competitive incursions into Greater Manchester during 1993, working into Bolton, Wigan and Manchester from their St Helens garage. The name Lancashire Travel was adopted, although not applied in this shot in Leigh that September. East Lancs-bodied Leyland Atlantean 1832 (TWM 216V) competes against GM Buses on the 582 service to Bolton.

Merseyside 0816 (F816 YLV), a 1989 MCW Metrobus, is pictured turning into Mosley Street in central Manchester in August 1994. MTL corporate livery is carried on this St Helens-based bus, including Lancashire Travel names.

Meanwhile, in Manchester, MTL set up a separate operation, MTL Manchester, initially drafting in a batch of East Lancs-bodied Atlanteans, painted in an orange and cream livery. 1732 (LKF 740R) enters Piccadilly in Manchester in October 1993, working the initial registered service: a marathon circular affair that linked Manchester with Bury and Rochdale.

The MTL Manchester operation expanded rapidly, and a large number of vehicles, mainly Leyland Nationals, were acquired. Former Ribble 6025 (FBV 525S) is seen in Mosley Street, in Manchester, in March 1994, wearing the new MTL group livery.

In addition to the used buses, MTL Manchester also received nine new Volvo B6/Plaxton. 7228 (L228 TKA) is seen in Corporation Street in May 1994 when new, competing against GM Buses North on the 135 and 136.

MTL also bought established independent Bolton Coachways, giving them an operating base in the town and an extra trading identity. D229 GLJ, an ex-Shamrock and Rambler Freight-Rover Sherpa/Dormobile, heads along Blackhorse Street in July 1994.

GM Buses South took retaliatory action against MTL by setting up Birkenhead & District, reviving corporation colours on a batch of Leyland Fleetlines. There was also an invasion into Liverpool, using conventional GMS-liveried Atlanteans. The Birkenhead contingent spent some weeks in Manchester on regular service out of Princess Road garage before deployment. 4020 (XBU 20S) demonstrates the attractive livery in this shot in Portland Street in May 1994.

GM Buses North also hit back against MTL, forming GMN Liverpool. The green-band and variant fleet name is demonstrated by Atherton-based Leyland Olympian 3280 (F280 DRJ). However, 3280 was actually on regular GMN duties in this view in Piccadilly bus station in April 1995. GMN also set up a minibus unit, Lancashire Gem, to compete in MTL territory in Southport.

GM Buses North purchased new Wright-bodied Volvo B10Bs in 1995 in their ongoing battle with MTL. They were proudly branded as 'Superbus', with colourful markings to denote innovative features. 510 (M510 PNA) is seen when new in Piccadilly bus station in February of that year. The 'low floor' legend was later amended to a more enigmatic 'floor line', as the B10B wasn't technically a true low-floor vehicle.

The scrap between MTL and the GM companies ended in June 1995, when a controversial deal was struck that restricted operators mainly to their own territory. The arrangement was later declared unlawful in a Monopolies and Mergers Commission investigation. A number of MTL buses passed to GMN as part of the deal. Leyland National 2 103 (XLV 163W), former Merseybus 6163, is pictured in GM North livery in Cannon Street, Manchester, that October.

It was no secret that Stagecoach had its eye on GM Buses South. The group targeted them by flooding the busy 192 route between Manchester and Hazel Grove with extra buses, operated by Ribble and branded as Stagecoach Manchester. Alexander-bodied Volvo B6s were initially used, later with larger B10Ms and occasionally drafted-in double-deckers on Saturdays. This scene in Stockport, in October 1994, is typical of the time, as Ribble 1418 (M418 RRN) heads up a long line of both operators' buses.

GM Buses South hit back at Stagecoach's 192 operation by registering competing journeys on Ribble's X43 service, using coaches from its Charterplan unit. One such vehicle was 100 (476 CEL), an ex-GMT Leyland Leopard, believed to be KDB 676P. The coach had been new in 1975 with an ECW body, and was subsequently rebodied by Duple, complete with wheelchair lift, in 1984. 100 leaves Manchester in June 1994 bound for Burnley.

Eventually, developments elsewhere in the country shaped Stagecoach's strategy in Manchester. The group's highly aggressive tactics during the takeover of Darlington brought much criticism and more scrutiny of their methods. Thus, conflict became courtship. Stagecoach leased out some of their Volvo B6 single-deckers to GMS, ostensibly as a business arrangement to modernise the GMS fleet. 307 (M743 PRS), new to Stagecoach Busways in November 1994, is seen in Stevenson Square the following May. The livery layout on these vehicles barely concealed their origins.

Stagecoach also sold its 192 registration and the Volvo B10Ms involved to Finglands. 1421 (M421 RRN) is pictured in Piccadilly in March 1996, with Finglands' colours applied to the existing Stagecoach zig-zag. Stagecoach had finally succeeded in their purchase of GMS the previous month; so the Atlantean on the 192 behind was, by then, competing against their former operation.

Chapter Four
The Drive Towards Low Floor

Accessibility was a major topic in the UK bus industry during the 1990s. There were calls to make access easier for wheelchair users, parents with children in buggies and those who would otherwise struggle with steps. Low-floor designs came onto the market, inspired by advancements in Europe, allowing step-free access from kerb to bus. In Greater Manchester, the PTE offered a kick-start grant to local operators to purchase new low-floor buses. In the end, market forces and passenger demand led to the movement growing further. Nowadays, of course, it is virtually the norm.

Before the availability of low-floor vehicles, GM Buses attempted to improve accessibility by having wheelchair lifts on the final two of its batch of ten new Volvo B10M/Northern Counties. Both were allocated to Oldham for use on service 408, on which 7009 (J709 ONF) is pictured working in June 1994, by that time owned by GM Buses North.

Timeline took six Volvo B10L under the GMPTE scheme, with bodywork by Alexander (Belfast), built under licence from a design by Swedish builder Säffle. 301 (N301 WNF) rests over at Moor Lane bus station in Bolton, when new in November 1995.

Pictured when new in Oldham, in November 1995, is GM Buses North 1071 (N71 YNF), a low-floor Volvo B6LE with Wright body. The bus carries similar branding to previous Volvo B10Bs and is operating service 408, a quantum leap away from the Volvo Citybus depicted on the service earlier.

Ribble specified unusual Berkhof bodywork on equally uncommon Dennis Lance SLF chassis for their GMPTE-supported low-floor buses, taking a batch of five in May 1995. 179 (N179 LCK) leaves Salford's Greengate arches when new.

Dennis's branched away from minibuses into low-floor single-deckers, taking several Plaxton-bodied Dennis Dart SLF. P742 HND stands outside Ashton Baths when new in August 1996.

Stuart's invested in two Dennis Dart SLF with East Lancs bodywork. 135 (P135 LNF) passes down Penny Meadow, in Ashton, when new in December 1996, shortly before the operator's demise the following year.

British Bus introduced low-floor Wright-bodied Scania L113 single-deckers for several of its Greater Manchester fleets during 1996. Five of these arrived that January for Arrowline, the Knutsford-based operator that had been acquired by the group. They were employed on two circular services, serving Altrincham and Manchester Airport, where 1004 (N104 YVU) is seen in June 1997.

Glossopdale took four examples of the Marshall Minibus in January 1997, in which month P458 EFL was photographed, approaching Tameside Hospital in Ashton. Reliability issues dogged this integral low-floor type throughout the industry, and Glossopdale had disposed of theirs by the following November.

Bluebird 20 (P20 BLU) was one of four Dennis Dart SLF with Wright bodies to enter service in June 1997, and is pictured in Piccadilly, Manchester, when new. Bluebird would invest heavily in low-floor vehicles in the following years.

Universal Buses Limited was initially a joint venture between Martin Bull, who owned Bu-Val, and Martin Wild, who had been with Citibus. The company obtained new, mainly low-floor, single-deckers and gained GMPTE schools and local service work, interworking such journeys with commercially registered services. R811 WJA, a UVG-bodied Dennis Dart SLF, is pictured in Rochdale in October 1997. Although the operation started brightly enough, in the end it floundered as contract work dried up and operational issues arose. The traffic commissioners eventually revoked Universal's operator licence in the early 2000s. Martin Bull, who had left Universal some years before this, continued to run Bu-Val.

Pictured in Wigan, in February 1998, is R643 MBV, working a GMPTE-supported 'Easylink' service. The bus was one of three ten-metre Optare Excel in the fleet of Tresize (Springfield Coachways).

Bullock became the first operator in Greater Manchester to run low-floor double-deckers, receiving two low-floor DAF DB250 with Optare's Spectra bodywork in March 1998. The pair were similar to examples provided to West Midlands Travel, including the livery layout, but with gold instead of blue. R290 CVM is pictured in Oxford Street, in Manchester, in April 1998. Bullock had already purchased five low-floor Scania L113CRL/Wright single-deckers just over two years previously, four of which had been acquired under the GMPTE scheme.

Mayne's had purchased five Marshall-bodied Dennis Dart SLF single-deckers in 1998 and followed this up with five Dennis Trident/East Lancs low-floor double-deckers in September 1999. 25 (V125 DJA) is pictured at the Broadoak in Ashton when new. The turquoise band – a throwback to Mayne's original bus livery – was initially applied to low-floor vehicles. Several weeks later, 25 suffered the indignity of being de-roofed in a low-bridge accident and was returned to East Lancs for repair.

UK North took delivery of four low-floor DAF DB250 with Alexander bodies, including V652 LWT, pictured in Manchester when new in September 1999. These were part of a dealer-stock batch that incorporated Transport for London features of the time, including the destination screen layout, for which UK North had bespoke blinds made.

Two new Mercedes-Benz O405N low-floor single-deckers arrived at Finglands in September 1999. 1428 (V428 DNB) was photographed in Manchester's Piccadilly bus station when new.

JP Travel took three Optare Solo minibuses with select registration marks in 1999. V4 JPT is seen turning into High Street, Manchester, that December.

Chapter Five
The Growing Presence of the Big Groups

The big groups – the likes of Stagecoach, British Bus and Badgerline – already had a major foothold in Greater Manchester in the nineties and, as the decade progressed, it became clear that this dominance was growing. GM Buses South was acquired by Stagecoach in February 1996; while First bought GM Buses North the following April. The creation of First in 1995, from the merger between Badgerline and GRT, meant that Badgerline's PMT-controlled Pennine fleet had already come under First's control. Elsewhere, British Bus sold out to Cowie Group in August 1996, with Cowie becoming Arriva the following year. A homogenised corporate livery was adopted, gradually eroding the previous colourful identities.

A cash-strapped Timeline sold out in two portions. The area, roughly, from south Manchester southwards into the Midlands passed to Arriva. Shortly afterwards, First acquired the other operations in the north and west of Greater Manchester.

There were also numerous operators who had, for one reason or another, fallen by the wayside, as is already described elsewhere.

Stagecoach finally achieved their aim of acquiring GMS, retaining the same Stagecoach Manchester name as its previous Ribble-operated venture. New vehicles were gradually introduced, such as 711 (N336 NPN), pictured when new in March 1996. This Alexander-bodied Volvo Olympian was diverted to Manchester from Stagecoach South Coast.

Stagecoach Manchester 1462 (FWH 462Y) stands in Piccadilly, Manchester, in this view from 1997. The bus was acquired with the GMS business, and was the second of two NCME-bodied Scania BR112DH, new to GMT in 1983. The Atlantean behind still carries GMS Buses livery and fleetnames, but with Stagecoach grey wheels added and, out-of-sight, the strapline 'A Stagecoach Subsidiary' underneath the name.

While still employee-owned, GM Buses South acquired and refurbished a large number of elderly Leyland Nationals for further service. These passed to Stagecoach at takeover, with a few receiving corporate livery. Perhaps the most notable was 265 (WFM 801K), seen in Stockport in January 1998. It had the honour of being the second production National built, when it entered service with Crosville in 1972.

Stagecoach Manchester introduced a 'Magic Bus' budget brand in 1996, reviving a name previously used in Scotland. Operation commenced using ex-GM Atlanteans, followed later by Olympians. However, the most memorable vehicles were twenty Dennis Dragons, bodied in Africa by AVA from kits built by Duple Metsec, which had been imported from Stagecoach Kenya in 1998. The first, 680 (M680 TDB), previously KAG 933E in Kenya, is seen in Parker Street, Manchester, that October.

Shortly after the takeover by First, former GM Buses North MCW Metrobus 5147 (SND 147X) received an experimental two-tone orange livery, as seen in this shot in Manchester in April 1996. The bus had been new to Greater Manchester Transport in 1982. The livery was not adopted.

In the end, First Greater Manchester adopted an all-over orange livery with blue lining. The new scheme is carried by Northern Counties-bodied Leyland Atlantean 4541 (ANA 541Y) in this view on Blackhorse Street in Bolton in May 1996.

First Greater Manchester took delivery of new Dennis Dart SLF and Volvo B10BLE in 1997, branded as 'Gold Service' and painted in a livery very similar to that employed already in Scotland. One of the Darts, Plaxton-bodied 6078 (R278 SBA), is pictured in Wigan in February 1998.

Officially, First's corporate livery was christened 'Willow Leaf', but to enthusiasts and staff alike it will always be 'Barbie', so named because of similar purple and pink shades employed on the packaging for the famous Mattel doll. Impressive arrivals in the scheme for First Manchester were fifteen articulated Volvo B10LA, purchased to upgrade the 135 service. 2003 (S993 UJA) is seen on Corporation Street, Manchester, in May 1999.

Bee Line eventually became Arriva Manchester. 697 (H667 GPF) stands on Mosley Street, in Manchester, in December 1998, demonstrating the group's corporate colours. This East Lancs-bodied Volvo B10M Citybus had been cascaded in from London, having been new to London & Country in 1990.

A special variation of Arriva's corporate livery is carried by 1073 (RDZ 1703), a Wright-bodied Scania N113CRL, new originally to London Buses in 1994. The bus is pictured arriving at Stretford Metrolink station in August 1999, on a shuttle service serving the Trafford Centre, at that time not linked into the Metrolink network. At the time of writing, construction work is underway to finally bring trams to the shopping centre.

H588 DVM, a former Timeline Alexander (Belfast)-bodied Volvo B10M in the Arriva North West fleet, is pictured leaving Manchester on the X4 service to Warrington in November 1998. The vehicle was originally new to Shearings in 1991.

Former Timeline 63 (G63 RND), a Leyland Tiger with Alexander (Belfast) bodywork, is pictured in Bolton in October 1998, shortly after the First takeover, with First markings added to the existing livery. The bus had been new to Shearings nine years earlier.

Whitehead sold his Pioneer operation to First, stipulating as part of the deal that it remain separate from the main First Manchester fleet. First Pioneer 1909 (HDZ 5433) stands on Cannon Street, in Manchester, in November 1999, carrying the same purple and yellow livery latterly used by Whitehead. This 1990 Wright-bodied Renault S75 was one of a batch transferred from London by First. Most were allocated into the main First Manchester fleet. The vehicles were widely disliked by drivers and fitters alike.

Demonstrating the First logo in this September 1997 shot in Ashton, is First Pennine IWC310 (F310 REH) – a Leyland Swift with uncompromising PMT bodywork. The bus has been drafted in from Stoke, as witnessed by the PMT name and 'Potteries Connection' branding.

A particularly exotic example in the First Pennine fleet was 700 (K174 EUX), a sole Volvo Olympian with Alexander Royale body, new to Singapore Bus Services as their SBS7204J. The single-door conversion is visible in this shot taken in October 1999, adjacent to First's Dukinfield garage. This had originally been Stuart's base.

Old versus new; little versus large. Despite the growth of the large corporates, there was still spirited competition going on. Both ends of the spectrum are shown in this view at Manchester University in May 1999. UK North's former GM Atlantean, MNC 507W, passes Stagecoach Manchester 156 (S156 TRJ), an Alexander-bodied MAN 18.220 that had been new the previous February.